Holiday Romance

Holiday Romance

Level 600 Reader (J)

Charles J. H. Dickens

Josh MacKinnon (Adaptation)
John McLean (Series Editor)

MATATABI PRESS

CHARLES J. H. DICKENS

Charles J. H. Dickens

Charles John Huffman Dickens was born in Portsmouth on the south coast of England in 1812. During his early years, he was a keen student, reading extensively. However, at the age of twelve, his formal education ended. His father was sent to prison because he owed money, and Charles was made to work to help pay it back. In spite of his lack of formal education, Charles went on to become one of the UK's best-known authors, writing fifteen novels, five novellas and hundreds of short stories. One of his most famous novellas, "A Christmas Carol," is as popular today as it was when it was first published in 1843. It has been transformed into numerous stage plays, films, and cartoons enjoyed by families around the world every year at Christmas.

Charles died in 1870 at the age of 58. He was buried in the Poets' Corner of Westminster Abbey.

Copyright © 2021 by MATATABI PRESS (910554), a subdivision of MATATABI HOLDINGS

All rights reserved. No part of this book may be reproduced in any manner whatsoever without written permission except in the case of brief quotations embodied in critical articles and reviews.

First Published: July 2021

MATATABI PRESS (910554)
Windwhistle, Farley Hill, Matlock. DE4 3LL. UK
20-20, 5-Chome, Yamamoto-shinmachi, Asaminami-ku, Hiroshima. 731-0139. JAPAN
https://www.press.matatabi-japan.com/
https://www.holdings.matatabi-japan.com/
Email: press@matatabi-japan.com
Tel: 0081-(0)70-8592-2501

ACKNOWLEDGEMENTS

Special thanks are due to the students from the Department of English at Yasuda Women's University in Hiroshima, Japan. In the final editing stages, they diligently checked and tested all four stories in this book to increase its suitability for EFL and ESL students worldwide.

CONTENTS

CHARLES J. H. DICKENS   v
ACKNOWLEDGEMENTS   ix

1 INTRODUCTORY ROMANCE BY WILLIAM TINKLING (Aged 8)   1

2 QUIZ (1)   15

3 ROMANCE BY NETTIE ASHFORD (Aged 6.5)   17

4 QUIZ (2)   32

5 ROMANCE BY ROBIN REDFORTH (Aged 9)   34

CONTENTS

6 | QUIZ (3) — 50

7 | ROMANCE BY ALICE RAINBIRD (Aged 7) — 52

8 | QUIZ (4) — 66

KEY VOCABULARY — 69
ANSWERS — 77
NOTE FROM THE PUBLISHER — 87
EDITORS — 93

1

INTRODUCTORY ROMANCE BY WILLIAM TINKLING (Aged 8)

The story I am going to tell you is true. Believe what I tell you if you want to understand the stories that follow. What's more, you must believe *everything* that I tell you. I, William Tinkling, am the editor of all four stories in this book.

Nettie Ashford is my wife. We first met at dance school. I used my pocket money to buy a green ring for her from a toyshop. We got married in the dance school closet in front of Robin Redforth, my cousin, and Alice Rainbird. After the ceremony, we went for a walk along the country road. Robin had a firework. He let it off to celebrate our marriage.

The next day, Robin and Alice got married in a similar way. This time, the firework made such a loud noise that a dog nearby started barking.

My lovely bride, Nettie, was a prisoner at Ms. Grimmer's house. Ms. Grimmer lived with her evil partner, Ms. Drowvey. Robin's lovely bride, Alice, was also a prisoner at their house. One day, Robin and I decided to free Nettie and Alice. We decided to do it the following week on Wednesday when they were out walking.

Robin loved danger. He suggested that we use fireworks to free our brides. Unfortunately, fireworks were too expensive, so we had to give up this plan.

At 2 p.m. on Wednesday, Robin came to my house. He was waving a black flag, and he had a paper knife hidden under his jacket. He had written a plan on a piece of paper. He had drawn me standing behind a streetlight. My ears were big and pointy, which they are *not*. Robin said that I must wait behind the streetlight until Drowvey falls to the ground. Then, I must rush out, get my bride, and fight my way to the country road. If necessary, I must fight to the death.

Drowvey, Grimmer, Nettie, and Alice appeared. Robin waved his black flag and attacked. I quietly waited behind the streetlight, but Drowvey didn't fall down. Far from it, she had wrapped Robin's head in his flag and was hitting him with an umbrella. Grimmer was angrily hitting him, too. Realizing that we had lost, I fought my way to the country road. Fortunately, I took the back route, so I didn't encounter anybody.

I waited and waited and waited for Robin. When he finally arrived, he said that our plan had failed because Drowvey had refused to fall down. She was too stubborn.

The next day at dance school, my beautiful bride silently walked up to me. She was very angry. She put a piece of paper into my hand. I opened it. "Is my husband a cow?"

A cow? Why would she call me a cow? What does this mean? At the end of the dance, I showed the piece of paper to Robin.

"She forgot to add a-r-d to the end of cow," he said.

"Cow, a-r-d?"

"Cow—cow—coward," he whispered in my ear. "She thinks that you were too scared to fight Drowvey and Grimmer."

A coward, I am *not*. I was *not* scared. I had to clear up my honour, so I demanded a trial in court. Robin agreed.

We had some difficulty arranging the trial. The Emperor of France's aunt, for example, had refused to let him leave the house. He had to escape over the back-wall of his garden.

HOLIDAY ROMANCE

British Library (1893)

The court was held on the grass by the pond.

My enemy, Richard, was there. I was led into the court by two guards. Nettie sat under an umbrella. Next to her was the President of the United States of America. He stood up and asked, "Coward, or no coward, guilty, or not guilty?"

I replied in a loud voice, "No coward, and not guilty." My enemy, Richard, stood up. He asked Alice if I had stayed behind the streetlight during the attack. Then, knowing it would hurt my feelings, he asked Nettie the same question.

Next, Robin entered the court. He was holding a piece of paper. This was what I'd been waiting for. I shook myself free from the guards. I asked Robin to tell everybody the most important thing during an attack. However, before he could answer, Richard shouted, "Bravery."

Richard's rudeness made the President of the United States of America very angry. He told the guards to put leaves into Richard's mouth. I watched with pleasure. Once again, I turned toward Robin. "Robin, what is the most important thing during an attack?" I asked. "Is it to follow orders?"

"It is," said Robin.

"Is that a piece of paper in your hand, Robin?" I asked.

"It is," said Robin.

"Is it the plan to free Nettie and Alice?"

"It is," said Robin.

"Please describe it. Then, give it to the President."

When the court heard that I'd followed orders, everybody cheered loudly. However, before the President could say the words, "No coward, and not guilty," The Emperor of France's aunt marched into the court. She grabbed the Emperor's hair and took him home. The court closed immediately.

The next evening, when the moonlight began to shine, Robin, Alice, Nettie, and I returned to where the trial had been held. We rested under a willow tree. Nettie and Alice silently stared at the pond. Some minutes passed without anybody speaking. Alice broke the silence. "We need to stop pretending," she said. "We need to give it up."

"Hah!" yelled Robin. "Pretending?"

"Don't, Robin. You worry me," replied Alice.

My lovely bride, Nettie, repeated Alice's comment. Robin and I looked at one another in silence.

"If," said Alice, "adults WON'T do what they should do, and WILL punish us, what can we gain from continuing to pretend?"

"We only get into trouble," said Nettie.

"Robin, you know very well," continued Alice, "that Ms. Drowvey wouldn't fall down. What's more, you know how embarrassingly the court ended. Now, think about our marriage. Do you really think my family will accept it?"

"Do you really think my family will accept our marriage, William?" said Nettie.

Robin and I looked at one another again.

"Robin, if you knocked at the door of my family home and claimed me," said Alice, "you would have your hair pulled, or your ears, or your nose."

"William, if you rang and rang my family home's doorbell and claimed me," said Nettie, "you would have things dropped on your head from the window."

"What about at your own homes?" continued Alice. "It would be just as bad. You would be sent to bed, or something equally embarrassing. What's more, how would you support us?"

Robin stood up. "By taking someone's property!" he yelled.

"What if the adults won't let you take their property?" said Alice.

"Then," said Robin, "I will make them pay a penalty in blood."

"What if they object?" said Alice. "What if they refuse to pay a penalty in blood or anything else?"

Everybody became silent.

"Do you still love me, Alice?" asked Robin.

"Robin Redforth! I am yours forever," replied Alice.

"Do you still love me, Nettie?" I asked.

"William Tinkling! I am yours forever," replied Nettie.

All four of us hugged. Now, don't misunderstand. Robin hugged Alice, and I hugged Nettie. However, two and two makes four.

"Nettie and I have been thinking," said Alice in a sad voice. "The adults are too strong for us. They make fools of us. Besides, they have changed our world. William Tinkling, your baby brother had a naming ceremony yesterday. Did a king attend the ceremony?"

"No," I replied.

"Were there any queens?" Nettie asked.

There had been no queens at our house. There might have been one in the kitchen. However, it was unlikely because no one had said anything about it.

"Any fairies?"

None that were visible.

"Did Grimmer come to the ceremony dressed like an evil witch and give your baby brother a bad gift?" asked Alice. "Answer, William."

Mother said that Uncle Chopper's gift was a poor quality one. However, she didn't say anything about it being a bad one.

HOLIDAY ROMANCE

Bradbury & Evans (1858)

"The adults have changed our world," said Alice.

"Evil criminals!" yelled Robin.

"No, Robin, Darling," said Alice, "don't call them such names. It won't help."

"There's only one thing that we can do," Alice said with a wise look on her face. "We must educate the adults. We must pretend in a different way. We must wait."

"How?" Robin yelled, angrily showing his teeth. He had four and a half teeth missing from the front. The last time he was taken to the dentist, he escaped before the other half of the tooth was removed. "How can we educate them? How can we pretend in a different way? How can we wait?" asked Robin.

"Tonight is our last night together, isn't it, Robin?" replied Alice. "Let's use this time to think about how we can educate the adults. Let's find a good way to tell them how to behave. William, you are the best and quickest writer, so you should write down what each of us thinks. Does everybody agree?"

"I guess so," replied Robin, "but how can we pretend in a different way?"

"Robin, we will continue to pretend," said Alice. "We will pretend to be children. However, we will stop pretending to be those adults who cannot understand us."

Robin was very unhappy. "How long do I have to wait?" he yelled.

HOLIDAY ROMANCE

Alice held Nettie's hand. She looked up at the sky. "We will wait without changing until the world changes. We will wait until adults stop making fools of us. We will wait until the fairies come back. If necessary, we will wait until we are 80, 90, or 100. Then, the fairies will send *us* children, and we will help the children ever so much."

"We will, Alice, Darling," said Nettie, hugging her. "Now, William, go and buy some cherries for us? I'll give you some money."

I asked Robin to come with me. However, he was far too angry. He was pulling up the grass and chewing it. When I came back with the cherries, however, Alice had helped him to calm down. She was comforting him by telling him how soon we would all be 90.

As we sat under the willow tree and ate the cherries, we pretended that we were 90. Nettie complained that a bone in her old back was painful. Alice sang a song in an old woman's way. It was very pretty. We were all happy.

We had too many cherries to eat. Alice had a tiny wineglass in her bag, so Alice and Nettie made some cherry-wine to celebrate our love.

Each of us had a glassful, and it was delicious. Alice raised her glass, "To *our love*," she said, drinking the cherry-wine. Robin drank his wine last. He had tears in his eyes.

I looked round and saw that there was nothing but moonlight under the willow tree. Nettie and Alice were gone. I burst into tears.

Robin and I were embarrassed about our red tearful eyes, so we stayed under the willow tree for 30 minutes until they returned to white. That evening, we imagined that we were 90. Robin said that he had a pair of boots that needed new heels. However, he was 90, so there was no point telling his father. A new pair of slippers would be far more useful. Robin said he felt that he was very old. His knees were beginning to feel painful. I told him the same. At dinner that night, everybody said that I was walking like an old man. I felt so pleased!

This is the end of the first story. This is the story that you should believe the most.

QUIZ (1)

1. Where did William Tinkling meet his wife, Nettie Ashford?
2. Where did Robin Redforth get married to Alice Rainbird?
3. What did Robin do to celebrate his marriage to Alice?
4. Who were Nettie and Alice staying with?
5. Why did Robin attack Ms. Grimmer and Ms. Drowvey?
6. What was Robin hiding under his jacket during the attack?
7. What did Ms. Drowvey wrap around Robin's head during the attack?
8. What did William do during the attack? Why?
9. Why did Robin's plan fail?

10. What was written on the piece of paper that Nettie gave to William?
11. Who had to escape over the back-wall of his garden to attend the trial?
12. Who was the judge during the trial?
13. What did the judge order the guards to do to William's enemy, Richard?
14. Why did the trial end early?
15. Where did William, Robin, Nettie and Alice go in the evening on the day after the trial?
16. What did Nettie and Alice say they had to stop doing? Why?
17. What did Alice say would happen if Robin went to her house and claimed her?
18. What did Nettie say would happen if William went to her house and claimed her?
19. What did they drink to celebrate their love?
20. Why did William and Robin stay under the willow tree after Nettie and Alice had gone home?

3

ROMANCE BY NETTIE ASHFORD (Aged 6.5)

There's a country where the children control everything. It's a wonderful country. Adults are called adult-children, and they must do everything the children say. Adult-children cannot stay up for late-night snacks, except on their birthdays. The children order them to make jam, jelly, cakes, pies and desserts. If the adult-children don't do as they're told, they're made to sit in a corner of the room. However, if they are good, they're *sometimes* given dessert.

CHARLES J. H. DICKENS

Cakes and Gâteaux showing various styles of Icing and Decoration.

Ms. Orange lived in this wonderful country. She was a sweet young girl. Unfortunately, her parents behaved badly every day. They had friends who were always causing trouble, too. One day, Ms. Orange said to herself, "These adult-children are too troublesome. I'm going to send them all to school."

Ms. Orange put on a beautiful dress and picked up her very heavy adult-baby. Then, she went to Ms. Lemon's house. Ms. Lemon was the head of a school for adult-children. Ms. Orange rang the doorbell.

The housecleaner answered.

"Good-morning," said Ms. Orange. "The weather is beautiful today, isn't it? May I speak to Ms. Lemon?"

"Yes, Madam."

"Please tell her that Nettie Orange is here with her adult-baby."

"Yes, Madam. Please come in. You can wait in the living room."

Ms. Lemon entered the living room. She was carrying a very heavy adult-baby. "Good morning, Ms. Lemon. The weather is beautiful today, isn't it? How are you, and how is your adult-baby?" asked Ms. Orange.

"Thank you for asking," Ms. Lemon replied. "I'm fine, but my adult-baby is a little sick. I think her teeth are hurting."

"Oh, I see," said Ms. Orange. "I hope she doesn't cry too much. How many teeth does she have?"

"Five," said Ms. Lemon, looking at her adult-baby's mouth.

"My adult-baby has eight," said Ms. Orange. "Let's put them down on the rug while we talk."

"Yes, let's do that," said Ms. Lemon. "They're so heavy."

"My first question, Ms. Lemon, is do you *have* any vacancies at your school?"

"Yes. How many do you require?"

"Well, Ms. Lemon, all eight of my adult-children are becoming too hard to control. I look after two parents, two of their close friends, one uncle, and three aunts. Do you have vacancies for eight adult-children?"

"I have exactly eight vacancies," said Ms. Lemon.

"That's excellent! Are the fees expensive?"

"No, the fees are very reasonable, Ms. Orange."

"Is the food good?"

"Yes, it's excellent," said Ms. Lemon.

"Do you hit the adult-children when they're bad?" asked Ms. Orange.

"Well, we occasionally hit them, but only when they've been very bad," said Ms. Lemon.

"Thank you. Can you show me around the school, Ms. Lemon?"

"Of course. Follow me, Ms. Orange."

Ms. Lemon took Ms. Orange into the schoolroom. "Stand up, Adult-children," said Ms. Lemon. All of the adult-children stood up.

"Why is the adult-boy with a red beard standing in the corner of the room? Has he done something wrong?" asked Ms. Orange.

Ms. Lemon called the adult-boy over. "Come here, Mr. White. Tell this lady why I made you stand in the corner of the room."

Charles Simon Pascal Soullier (1861)

"I've been gambling, Madam," said Mr. White.

"Are you sorry for what you did?" asked Ms. Lemon.

"No, I'm *not*," he yelled. "I only feel sorry when I lose money."

"He's a bad one," said Ms. Lemon. "Return to the corner, Mr. White, and stay there until you're ready to apologize."

Ms. Lemon pointed to another adult-boy. "That's Mr. Brown. He has a very serious problem. He eats and drinks too much. He's greedy. How are your knees today, Mr. Brown?"

"Very painful," replied Mr. Brown.

"Well, it's because you're overweight, Mr. Brown," said Ms. Lemon. "Your stomach is the size of two stomachs. Go and exercise right now."

Next, Ms. Lemon pointed to an adult-girl. That's Ms. Black. She's always running around, getting her clothes dirty. "Come here, Ms. Black. Well, Ms. Black, are you going to improve your behaviour?"

"I don't want to improve my behaviour," yelled Ms. Black. "I just don't *want* to!"

"She won't take advice from anybody, and she gets angry so quickly," said Ms. Lemon. "If you watch her running around laughing, you might think she's cheerful and friendly. However, she's as bad as the worst of them!"

"Looking after all of these troublesome adult-children must be such hard work," said Ms. Orange.

"It is. It is," said Ms. Lemon. "They're always yelling and complaining about something. They argue with one another all day long. The worst thing they do is to bully. They all want to believe that they're better than everybody else."

"Thank you, Ms. Lemon. It was very kind of

you to show me around your school. I'll go home now and get my adult-children ready to come here," said Ms. Orange.

"It was my pleasure, Ms. Orange. I'll make sure that their beds are ready when they arrive," said Ms. Lemon.

Ms. Orange picked up her adult-baby and went home. As soon as she arrived at the house, she told her adult-children to pack their bags. They refused, of course, but it was no good. Ms. Orange took them to the school, wished them good luck, and waved goodbye.

"How wonderful! I can finally take a rest!" said Ms. Orange, sitting down on her armchair.

Just then, Ms. Ali rang Ms. Orange's doorbell.

"Ms. Ali," said Ms. Orange, "it's lovely to see you. Please come in. I'm about to eat lunch. Join me. I'm having some sweet stuff followed by a dish of sweet bread and sweet dessert?"

"Thank you so much, Ms. Orange. Actually, I came to invite you to a party," said Ms. Ali.

"A party?" said Ms. Orange.

"Yes, we're having a small party at our house tonight for all of the adult-children in the neighbourhood. I hope that you, Mr. Orange, and your adult-baby can join us."

"Yes! We'd love to!" said Ms. Orange.

"Excellent!" said Ms. Ali.

Just then, Mr. Orange came home from the city.

"William, Darling," said Ms. Orange, "you look tired. Did you have a busy day in the city?"

"Yes, I was pushing and pulling tables all day long, Nettie," said Mr. Orange. "It was such hard work."

"What a terrible place to work, William," said Ms. Orange, gently pressing his arm.

Lunch was ready. They sat down to eat. Mr. Orange cut the sweet stuff into slices. "Let's celebrate," he said. "Nettie, Darling, bring a bottle of our best ginger-beer."

In the evening, Mr. and Ms. Orange, and their adult-baby went to Ms. Ali's house. Ms. Ali had decorated her living room with paper flowers.

"How beautiful!" said Ms. Orange. The adult-children will be so happy."

Mr. Orange looked at the decorations. "I'm

not really interested in adult-children," he said, shaking his head.

"Surely, you like adult-girls," said Ms. Ali.

Mr. Orange shook his head. "They all think that they are more important than everybody else."

"William, Darling, look at this," said Ms. Orange "Isn't it wonderful! Ms. Ali has prepared dinner for the adult-children. Here's their little salmon! Here's their little salad, their little roast beef, and their tiny, tiny, tiny glasses of champagne!"

"I think it's best if the adult-children have dinner in the back room by themselves," said Ms. Ali. "Our table is in the corner over here."

The adult-children started to arrive. The first was an overweight adult-boy. He was wearing glasses. The housecleaner brought him in. "Hello, come in," said Ms. Ali. "Take a seat at that table over there. Someone will bring you a drink."

Next, more adult-children arrived. Some of them started to behave badly as soon as they entered the house. They were walking around with cups of tea or coffee in their hands. Four very fat and very boring adult-boys were standing in the doorway, talking about newspapers. Ms. Ali scolded them. "Boys, no one can get in or out of the house if you stand there. Move or I will send you home." One adult-boy with a beard was standing on the rug in front of the fire. He was warming his back. Ms. Ali sent him home first. "Your behaviour is very bad," she said, pushing him out of the house.

A band started to play music. One adult-child played the harp; one played the cornet; and one, the piano. Ms. Ali and Ms. Orange told the adult-children to find a dance partner. Many of the adult-boys refused to dance. Some of them politely said, "Not now, maybe later," while others loudly yelled, "I *never* dance!"

"These adult-children are so stubborn! Looking after them is such hard work," said Ms. Ali to Ms. Orange.

"I agree. They're lovely, but they really are troublesome," said Ms. Orange to Ms. Ali.

After some time, the adult-children became a little quieter. Some of the adult-boys started to slide around the dance floor. However, they still refused to dance.

The adult-boys were so troublesome. First, they refused to sing. Then, all of a sudden, they would start singing. "If you continue to behave badly," said Ms. Ali to a tall adult-boy, "I'll send you to bed immediately."

The adult-girls were wearing very long dresses. In fact, they were so long that they dragged along the floor. The adult-boys kept accidently standing on the dresses. Whenever this happened, the adult-girls angrily yelled, screamed and shook their fists.

One thing that made everybody happy was when Ms. Ali yelled, "Dinner is ready!" All of the adult-children ran to the table, pushing and yelling at one another.

"How are the adult-children getting on, Darling?" Mr. Orange asked Ms. Orange.

"Oh, they're having a wonderful time, Darling!" said Ms. Orange. "It makes me laugh to see them trying to impress one another! Come and look!"

"Darling," said Mr. Orange, "you know that I'm not interested in adult-children."

Ms. Orange placed her adult-baby on the floor next to Mr. Orange and returned to watch the adult-children.

"What are they doing now?" said Ms. Orange to Ms. Ali.

"They're making speeches. They're pretending to be politicians," said Ms. Ali.

Ms. Orange returned to talk to Mr. Orange. "William, Darling, please come and look. The adult-children are pretending to be politicians."

"Darling," said Mr. Orange, "you know I'm not interested in politics."

Once again, Ms. Orange returned to watch the adult-children. When she entered the room, some of the adult-boys were yelling, "Yes, yes, yes!" Others were yelling, "No, no, no!" and some were simply yelling whatever they were thinking about at that time. One of the very fat and very boring adult-boys stood up and started to explain something very boring. After a very long time, he sat down. Then, another fat and boring adult-boy stood up and made another long and boring speech. Finally, one of the troublesome fat adult-boys raised his drinking glass. "To Ms. Ali!" he yelled. "Thank you for a wonderful party." Everybody cheered loudly.

Some adult-boys started making speeches again, so Ms. Ali clapped her hands loudly. "Now, you've enjoyed pretending to be politicians. However, it's getting late. You can have one more dance. Then, you must all go home."

After the final dance, children came to take their adult-children home. Luckily, the two fat and boring adult-boys who had made very boring speeches were taken home first.

When they were all gone, Ms. Ali sat down on the sofa. "Looking after adult-children is such hard work, Ms. Orange," she said.

"They're lovely," replied Ms. Orange. "However, they really are troublesome"

Mr. and Ms. Orange put on their hats, picked up their adult-baby, and started to walk home. They passed in front of Ms. Lemon's school.

"I wonder, William, Darling," said Ms. Orange, looking up at the window. "I wonder if our lovely adult-children are asleep!"

"I really don't care what they're doing," said Mr. Orange.

"William, Darling!"

"You think about them all the time, don't you?" said Mr. Orange.

"Yes, I do," said Ms. Orange. "I really do!"

"Well, I don't," said Mr. Orange.

"William, Darling," said Ms. Orange, pressing his arm, "I've got an idea. Do you think Ms. Lemon will let the adult-children stay at school throughout the holidays?"

"I'm sure she will if we pay her," said Mr. Orange.

"I love spending time with our adult-children, William," said Ms. Orange, "but it's probably better for them to stay with Ms. Lemon. Let's pay her to keep them throughout the holidays."

That was what made this such a wonderful country. Soon, all of the adult-children were sent away to school during the holidays. They were kept in school for as long as they lived, and they were made to do whatever the children told them to do.

4

QUIZ (2)

1. List five things that children ordered adult-children to make.
2. Where were adult-children made to sit if they didn't do as they were told?
3. Who was the principal of the school for adult-children?
4. Why do you think adult-babies have so few teeth?
5. Where did Ms. Orange and the school principal put their adult babies while they were talking?
6. List all of the adult-children that Ms. Orange took care of.
7. Why was Mr. White made to stand in the corner of the room?
8. What was Mr. Brown's serious problem?

9. What did the principal say was the worst thing that adult-children did?
10. What did Ms. Orange eat for lunch?
11. Who ate lunch with Ms. Orange?
12. What decorations did Ms. Ali put in her living room?
13. What did Mr. Orange say about adult-girls?
14. What food did Ms. Ali prepare for the adult-children?
15. Describe the first adult-child to arrive at the party.
16. What were the adult-boys who were standing in the doorway talking about?
17. Why did Ms. Ali send the adult-boy with a beard home early?
18. What instruments did the band play?
19. What were the adult children who were making speeches pretending to be?
20. Where were the adult-children sent during the holidays?

5

ROMANCE BY ROBIN REDFORTH (Aged 9)

Captain Braveheart is a famous pirate. He's also the writer and hero of this story. The captain became a pirate when he was nine years old. Now, he owns a huge and powerful ship named *The Beauty*. It has 100 guns.

Before becoming a pirate, the captain was an ordinary schoolchild. One day, however, his Latin teacher was feeling angry. The teacher scolded the captain very badly for no reason. To keep his honour, the captain challenged the teacher to a fight. When the teacher refused, the captain bought an old handgun, put some sandwiches in a paper bag, made a strong drink, and became a pirate.

HOLIDAY ROMANCE

Cornelis Ploos van Amstel (1759)

On a lovely summer's day, the captain was sailing *The Beauty* in the South China Sea. His sailors were sitting around him. Everybody was singing.

Life on land is not for me!
Out on the sea, I feel so free!
Hey, hey, heave-ho!
Hey, hey, heave-ho!

Suddenly, a sailor yelled, "Whales!"

Sir Albert Hastings Markham (1894)

"Where are they?" yelled Captain Braveheart, jumping to his feet.

"On the front left side, Captain," replied the

sailor, touching his hat to show respect. All of the sailors knew it was very important to show respect to the captain. Anybody who forgot to show respect was thrown into the sea.

"This adventure belongs to me," said Captain Braveheart, getting into a small boat.

The sailors became very excited.

"Captain's near the whales!" said an elderly sailor, watching with his telescope.

"He's caught something!" said a young sailor, pointing out to sea.

"He's dragging it this way!" said another sailor, jumping up and down.

The captain approached *The Beauty*, dragging a whale through the water. All of the sailors yelled, "Braveheart! Braveheart!" The sailors lifted the whale onto *The Beauty*. It was huge.

"Raise the sails, Men," Captain Braveheart ordered. "We're going North West." They sailed at high speed over the deep blue sea.

Nothing special happened for two weeks. Well, nothing special for pirates happened. They captured and stole treasure from four Spanish ships and one South American ship...nothing special for pirates. The sailors were beginning to feel bored. They wanted more action and adventure.

Captain Braveheart ordered everybody to come to the middle of the ship. "Men, I hear that some of you are unhappy," he yelled. "If you want to complain about something, come forward now!"

After some time, Bill Boozey came forward. He was a huge, strong man. However, when the captain looked at him, his legs became weak.

"Speak up! What do you want to say to me?" yelled the captain, taking out his handgun.

Mary Orvis Marbury (1892)

"Well, err, well, Captain Braveheart," replied

Bill Boozey, his voice shaking. "I've sailed on ships my whole life. Err, well, err, the milk in our tea on this ship is the worst I've ever ta..."

Just as Bill Boozey was saying the word "tasted," he noticed that the captain was holding his handgun. Bill stepped backward and fell into the sea. Unfortunately, he couldn't swim.

The sailors were shocked.

Captain Braveheart took off his coat and jumped into the sea. Saving such a huge man was not very easy. The captain took hold of Bill Boozey's shirt and dragged him back to the ship. The sailors cheered loudly. From that day on, Bill Boozey became the captain's most trustworthy sailor.

Captain Braveheart pointed at a ship in the distance. It was in a harbour. "We'll capture that ship tomorrow at dawn," he said. "Everybody can have a big glass of alcohol tonight."

In the morning, the ship, which was called *The Scorpion*, sailed out of the harbour. It fired a gun at *The Beauty*. Then, it raised a flag. It was the Latin teacher's flag.

Captain Braveheart spoke to his sailors. "Capture the Latin teacher alive," he ordered. "Now, get ready for battle, Men."

The fight began. *The Beauty* repeatedly fired its guns at *The Scorpion*. *The Scorpion* fired its guns at *The Beauty*. However, *The Beauty* was much faster and much more powerful than *The Scorpion*.

The Latin teacher was encouraging his men to fight harder. Clearly, he was a brave man. However, his clothes—his white hat, his short trousers, and his long school coat—were nothing compared to Captain Braveheart's fashionable uniform.

The two ships were side by side. Captain Braveheart jumped onto *The Scorpion*. His sailors followed.

A fight started. When the Latin teacher saw that his men were beaten, he put down his gun and raised his hands. The captain's sailors captured the Latin teacher. They took him to *The Beauty*. *The Scorpion* sank to the bottom of the sea.

The sailors gathered around the Latin teacher. The cook was particularly angry. His brother had been killed in the battle. He ran toward the Latin teacher with a cooking knife in his hand. The captain fired his handgun and killed the cook.

Captain Braveheart approached the Latin teacher. He pushed him to the ground. Then, he turned toward his sailors. "How should we punish him for scolding a schoolchild for no reason, Men?" he asked.

All the sailors yelled, "Death!"

"Yes, I agree, Men. He deserves to die," said the captain. "However, we are honourable pirates. It would be dishonourable to kill him." The captain thought for a moment. "Prepare one of the small boats!" he ordered.

A boat was immediately prepared.

"I'm not going to kill you," said the captain. "However, I will never let you scold schoolchildren again. Get in this boat. You have a compass, a bottle of alcohol, a bottle of water, a piece of pork, a bag of biscuits, and my Latin grammar book. Go to a nearby island, and live with the natives."

The unhappy Latin teacher got into the boat. He lay on his back and looked up at the sky. *The Beauty* sailed away.

A strong wind began to blow. *The Beauty*

sailed South West. Captain Braveheart was tired after the battle. He had cuts all over his body, so he went to his room to rest and recover.

The next morning, the weather turned bad. Thunder and lightning continued for six weeks. Then, hurricanes followed by tornadoes blew for two months. The oldest sailor on *The Beauty* said that it was the worst weather he'd ever seen.

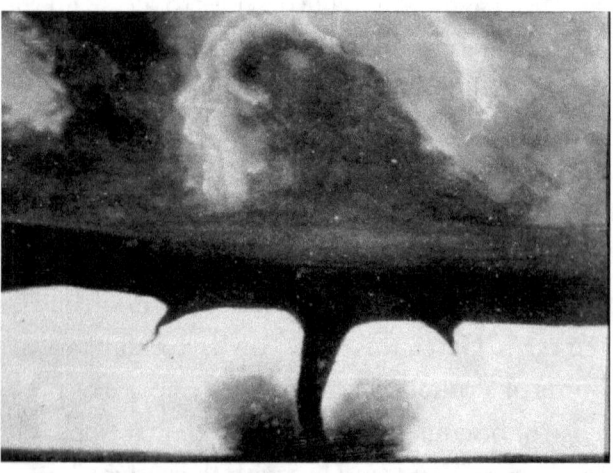

National Oceanic & Atmospheric Administration (NOAA) Photo Library

Food was running out. The captain reduced everybody's food by half. Then, he reduced his own food even more. Bill Boozey noticed that the captain was eating less than everybody else was. "Captain, you need to eat," he said. "Let me kill myself. Then, you can eat my body."

"You're a good man, Bill Boozey," said the captain. "Thank you, but no thank you."

When the men were too weak to stand, a miracle happened. The sky became blue. "Land!" a sailor yelled.

"Natives!" another yelled.

Hundreds of natives were approaching *The Beauty* in canoes. They were singing loudly.

Chew-a-chew-a-chew tooth.
Munch, munch. Nice!
Chew-a-chew-a-chew tooth.
Munch, munch. Nice!

It soon became clear that the natives were planning to chew, munch and eat the sailors. The chief of the natives, who spoke excellent English, was the first to get onto *The Beauty*. He raised his arm to tell the others to attack. Then, Captain Braveheart walked toward him. When the chief saw the captain, he immediately called off the attack. He'd heard many stories about Captain Braveheart. The chief shook in fear. "Please don't kill us," he said, going down onto his hands and knees in front of the captain. The captain told the chief to stand up and promised not to hurt him.

The natives prepared a huge meal for the sailors. After eating, the chief invited Captain Braveheart to his village. The captain accepted the invitation. However, he did not trust the chief, so he told his sailors to keep their guns ready.

When they arrived at the chief's village, the captain was surprised to see the Latin teacher. The natives had shaved his head, tied him to a tree, and put flour all over his body. They were planning to eat him.

Captain Braveheart spoke to his sailors. "The Latin teacher is a very bad man," he said. "However, we cannot leave an Englishman to be cooked and eaten by the natives." The sailors agreed. They decided to save the Latin teacher on two conditions:

1. *He promises to never teach again; and*

2. *He spends the rest of his life doing Latin homework for schoolchildren.*

Captain Braveheart freed the Latin teacher. "Get ready for battle, Men," he said, raising his handgun. The natives started yelling when they saw that the captain had freed the Latin teacher. They angrily ran toward the sailors. "Fire your guns, Men!" ordered Captain Braveheart. "Fire! Fire! Fire!"

Hundreds of natives were killed. Hundreds were injured, and thousands ran into the forest to hide. After defeating the natives, the sailors took the Latin teacher to *The Beauty*.

This time, they sailed to a friendly island where the natives ate vegetables and pork. The chief on this island was very kind. He gave Captain Braveheart food, spices, and jewels.

When the sun came up on the third day, the captain pointed out to sea. "Raise the sails, Men!" he ordered. "We're going to England." All of the sailors cheered loudly.

After months on the open sea, *The Beauty* approached the southern coast of Spain. A ship sailed toward them. Captain Braveheart recognized its flag. It was the flag from his garden in England. It was his father's ship, *The Family*.

Bill Boozey rowed a small boat to *The Family*. When he returned, his boat was full of presents of fresh meat and vegetables. The captain's mother, father, aunts, uncles and cousins were on *The Family*. They all wanted to hug Captain Braveheart and take him home. However, the captain did not want to return home. Instead, he invited his family to a party on *The Beauty* the next day.

That night, the Latin teacher used a flashlight to send a message to *The Family*. He said that he would help them capture the captain and take him home. The sailors caught the Latin teacher. The next morning, the Latin teacher was thrown into the sea for behaving dishonestly.

The party was a great success. It started at ten in the morning and continued until seven the next morning. The captain's parents were so happy to see him that they cried tears of joy. His uncles, aunts, and cousins were amazed by the size of *The Beauty*. The captain ordered his men to fire all 100 of the ship's guns. His cousin, Tom, became excited and started to behave badly. The captain's men locked Tom in a room for a few hours to keep him quiet.

Captain Braveheart invited his mother to his private room. "Where is my bride, Alice Rainbird?" he asked. His mother said that she was staying in the seaside town of Margate. However, Alice's family did not want her to marry the captain. The captain became very angry. He ran out of the room. "Raise the sails, Men," he ordered. "We're going to Margate to save Alice Rainbird."

Margate Harbour (1890-1900)

When they arrived at Margate, the captain rowed a small boat to the beach. His sailors followed. William Tinkling, the captain's honourable and brave cousin, led the sailors. The captain spoke to the mayor.

"Do you know the name of my ship, Mayor?" the captain asked.

"No," said the mayor, rubbing his eyes.

"It's *The Beauty*," said the captain.

"Oh! Oh! I'm sorry," said the mayor, looking shocked. "Are you the famous Captain Braveheart?"

"I am!"

The mayor started to shake in fear. He'd heard many stories about Captain Braveheart.

"Now, Mayor," said the captain, "help me save my bride, Alice Rainbird. If you don't help, I will attack Margate."

The mayor went to look for Alice. Bill Boozey went with him.

After two hours, the mayor and Bill Boozey returned. "Captain," said the mayor, "Alice is getting ready to go for a swim in the sea. When she enters the sea, I will help you to rescue her."

"Mayor," said Captain Braveheart, "you have saved your town."

The captain waited near the beach. When Alice entered the sea, the mayor rowed his boat to one side of her. The captain rowed his boat to her other side. Alice was confused. She screamed in fear. Captain Braveheart put his strong arms around Alice. He pulled her onto his boat. Alice's fear turned to joy. The captain took her to *The Beauty*.

Soon after, the mayor rang the harbour bells. It was a signal for the captain. Alice's family had agreed to let her marry the captain. A boat from the church arrived. The captain and Alice got married.

Captain Braveheart gave expensive gifts to everybody on *The Family*. They all loved the gifts. Unfortunately, the captain's cousin, Tom, became excited and started to behave badly again, so he was locked in a room to keep him quiet. However, Alice soon let him out. The sailors raised the sails on *The Beauty*. It departed for the Indian Ocean. The captain and Alice enjoyed a long and happy life together.

6

QUIZ (3)

1. Why did Captain Braveheart become a pirate?
2. What was Captain Braveheart's ship called?
3. What did Captain Braveheart catch in the South China Sea?
4. What happened during the two weeks when *nothing special happened*?
5. Why was Bill Boozey unhappy about the tea?
6. What happened to Bill Boozey when he was telling the captain about the tea?
7. What was the ship in the harbour called?
8. Who was the captain of the ship in the harbour?
9. Why did the cook run toward the Latin teacher with a cooking knife in his hand?

HOLIDAY ROMANCE

10. Why do you think Captain Braveheart killed the cook?
11. What did Captain Braveheart give the Latin teacher after putting him in a boat?
12. Describe the bad weather that continued for approximately three and half months.
13. What did the natives that approached *The Beauty* in canoes want to do to the sailors?
14. Who did Captain Braveheart find in the natives' village?
15. What did the sailors do when Captain Braveheart told them they were going to sail to England?
16. Who was on the ship named *The Family*?
17. Why did the sailors throw the Latin teacher into the sea?
18. Who did the sailors lock in a room? Why?
19. Why did Captain Braveheart sail to Margate?
20. Why did the mayor ring the harbour bells?

ROMANCE BY ALICE RAINBIRD (Aged 7)

Once upon a time, there was a king and a queen. The king was strong, brave, and handsome. The queen was intelligent, beautiful and kind. They had nineteen children. The eldest, Alice, was seven years old. She took care of her younger brothers and sisters.

One day, while the king was walking to his office, he stopped at the fish market. He bought some salmon and enjoyed talking to the store-owner. Then, he continued on his way. A few minutes later, a young boy came running toward him. "Excuse me, Sir!" the boy said. "There was an old woman staring at you at the fish market. Did you see her?"

Samuel Kilbourne (1879)

The king was surprised. "What old woman?" he said. "I was the only customer."

Just then, the old woman from the fish market came running toward the king. She was wearing expensive silk, and she smelled of dried lavender.

"Are you King Rainbird?" asked the old woman.

"Yes, that's my name," replied the king.

"Is your daughter the beautiful Princess Alice?" asked the old woman.

"Yes, Alice is the eldest of my nineteen children," replied the king.

"I am a good fairy," said the old woman. "My name is Marina. When you return home for dinner this evening, politely offer Princess Alice some of the salmon you bought."

"What if she doesn't want it?" said the king.

Fairy Marina became very angry. "Don't be so greedy!" she yelled. "I know you want to eat it all by yourself."

The king lowered his head. "Please forgive me," he said.

"Be good, then," said Fairy Marina. "When Princess Alice eats the salmon, she will leave the bone on her plate. Tell her to dry it, rub it, and polish it until it shines. It's a present from me."

"Is that all?" asked the king.

"One more thing," said Fairy Marina, "the fishbone is magic. Princess Alice can use it to wish for whatever she wants. However, she can only use it once after trying very hard and after trying everything."

The king started to ask a question. "Why…"

Fairy Marina angrily kicked the ground. "Adults are *always* asking why. Why! Why! Why!" she yelled, staring at him. "Well, there is no reason!"

The king shook in fear. He promised never to

ask why again. Fairy Marina flew away, and the king continued walking to his office.

In the evening, the king politely offered Princess Alice some salmon. She accepted his offer. She enjoyed it very much. When she had finished eating, the only thing on her plate was the fishbone. The king told Princess Alice what Fairy Marina had said.

Princess Alice dried the bone, rubbed it, and polished it. It shone like a pearl.

The next morning, when the queen got out of bed, she put her hands on her head. "Oh, dear me, dear me. My head, my head, it hurts so much!" she said, falling to the ground.

Princess Alice ran to help the queen. She took the fishbone out of her pocket. However, when she started to wish for her mother's health, she noticed a jar of strong smelling herbs next to the bed. She carefully put the fishbone back into her pocket. Then, she held the jar under the queen's nose. The queen opened her eyes. "Don't worry, Mother. I'll look after you," Princess Alice said, pressing a wet towel on the queen's head.

The queen was very sick. Princess Alice took

good care of her and all of the young princes and princesses. She dressed and undressed the baby prince. She boiled the kettle for tea, heated soup, swept the floor, and prepared the queen's medicine. She was busy from first thing in the morning to last thing at night. What's more, there were no cooks or cleaners to help because the king was too poor to employ them.

Princess Alice had a close friend, Little Lady. She told Little Lady all of her secrets. She was a good listener. To other people, Little Lady was just a doll. To Princess Alice, however, she was more than a doll. When Alice told her about the fishbone, Little Lady smiled and nodded. She only did this when she was alone with Princess Alice.

In the evenings, Princess Alice and the king took care of the queen together. The king was always angry. He wanted Alice to use her fishbone to make the queen better. Whenever the king became angry, Alice ran to her room to talk to Little Lady. "Adults think we never have a reason for doing things," she said, holding Little Lady. Little Lady smiled.

"Alice," said the king one evening.

"Yes, Father."

"Have you lost your magic fishbone?" he asked.

"No, it's in my pocket, Father!"

"Oh, I thought you'd lost it?"

"Of course not, Father."

Conradijn Cunaeus (1880–1895)

Princess Alice took very good care of the queen. One day, for example, the noisy dog that lived next door tried to bite one of the young princes. As the prince ran away from the dog, he fell and cut his hand on some glass. There was so much blood. The other princes and princesses were shocked. They all started crying loudly. Princess Alice was worried that the noise would wake the queen, so she quickly put her hands over their mouths to keep them quiet. Then, she gently washed the blood from the young prince's hand and put a bandage on it.

The king quietly watched Alice. "Alice," he said.

"Yes, Father."

"What have you been doing?" he asked.

"Cleaning and bandaging, Father."

"Have you lost your magic fishbone?" he asked.

"No, it's in my pocket, Father!"

"Oh, I thought you'd lost it?"

"Of course not, Father."

After that, Princess Alice ran to her room to talk to Little Lady. She told her what her father had said. Little Lady laughed.

Well, another time, while Princess Alice was making soup for dinner, her youngest brother, the baby prince, fell down the stairs. He injured his eye. The other young princes and princesses were shocked when they saw his eye. They all started crying loudly. Princess Alice was worried that the noise would wake the queen. She ran to the baby prince, picked him up, checked that he was okay, and gently rocked him to sleep. Next, she told the other princes and princesses to come to the kitchen. They all stopped crying and excitedly ran to the kitchen. While holding the baby prince, she taught the other princes and princesses how to make soup. They all enjoyed making soup. Then, they enjoyed eating it together.

The king quietly watched Alice. "Alice," he said.

"Yes, Father."

"What have you been doing?" he asked.

"Cooking and cleaning, Father."

"Have you lost your magic fishbone?" he asked.

"No, it's in my pocket, Father!"

"Oh, I thought you'd lost it," he said.

"Of course not, Father."

The king sighed. He looked so sad. "Are you

okay, Father?" Alice asked, putting her hand on his shoulder.

"I am so very, very poor, Alice," he said.

"How much money do you have, Father?" Princess Alice asked.

"None," he said, sighing again.

"Is there no way for you to get money, Father?"

"No," said the king, lowering his head. "I have tried very hard, and I have tried everything."

Princess Alice put her hand into her pocket. "Father, please be honest. Have you really tried very hard? Have you really tried everything?" she asked.

"Yes, Alice. I have."

"Well," she said, sitting down next to him, "if you cannot succeed after trying very hard and after trying everything, you can ask for help. That's the secret of the fishbone."

Princess Alice gently kissed the fishbone. "Please make today *bonus day* for my father," she said. "He has tried very hard, and he has tried everything."

Princess Alice heard a loud noise coming from the garden. Money was falling from the sky. Alice and her father ran outside. Just then, Fairy Marina came flying through the sky on a carriage pulled by four beautiful birds. She was wearing silk, and she smelled of dried lavender.

Rolland Ayres (1935–1942)

"Princess Alice," said Fairy Marina, "it's lovely to see you. Come here, and give me a hug." Alice ran up to Fairy Marina and gave her a big hug. Fairy Marina looked at the king. "How are you, King Rainbird?" she asked.

CHARLES J. H. DICKENS

The king smiled. "I'm much better now, thank you," he said, bowing.

"Do you understand why Princess Alice did not use her fishbone to help the queen?" asked Fairy Marina. "Do you understand why Princess Alice did not use her fishbone to help the young prince and her baby brother?"

The king's face turned red. "Yes, now I understand," he said, nervously bowing again.

"Ah! *Now* you understand, but you didn't understand *then*, did you?" yelled Fairy Marina.

The king nervously bowed again. "No, I'm very sorry," he said, looking at Princess Alice.

"Be good, and be happy, then," said Fairy Marina.

Fairy Marina opened her magic fan. The queen and all the princes and princesses suddenly appeared. They were wearing beautiful clothes and were laughing and smiling. Next, Fairy Marina touched Princess Alice's shoulder with her fan. Alice's old clothes changed into a beautiful silk dress and golden bows appeared on her shoes.

Fairy Marina opened the door of her carriage. "After you, Princess Alice," she said. "A handsome young prince is waiting for you at the church." A smile spread across Princess Alice's face. Next, Fairy Marina spoke to the king, the queen, and all of the princes and princesses. "Join us at the church in exactly 30 minutes," she said.

The carriage flew up into the sky and headed toward the church. A handsome young prince called Robin was sitting alone in the church garden. He was eating a sugar cube, waiting to be 90 years old.

When Prince Robin saw the carriage flying through the sky, he knew something special was about to happen. "Prince Robin," said Fairy Marina, "I have brought your bride." A smile spread across Prince Robin's face. Fairy Marina touched Prince Robin's shoulder with her fan. His clothes became new, his hair became neat, and his old hat flew away.

Princess Alice and Prince Robin entered the church. Their family, friends and neighbours were waiting inside. Everybody cheered loudly.

The wedding ceremony was beautiful. Afterwards, everybody enjoyed a delicious wedding meal. The room was decorated with white ribbons and white flowers.

When the desserts were served, Fairy Marina stood up. She raised her drinking glass. "Let's drink to celebrate the marriage of a beautiful couple," she said. "I hope they have a long and happy life together." Next, Prince Robin stood up. He made an emotional speech. Everybody cried tears of joy and yelled *hooray*.

Fairy Marina approached the king and queen. She told them that they would never be poor again. What's more, from now on, the king would receive eight bonuses a year. Then, Fairy Marina spoke to Princess Alice and Prince Robin. "Darlings, you will have 35 beautiful children, seventeen boys and eighteen girls. They will all have beautiful curly hair, and they will all be very good and healthy. They will never catch a cold or get sick."

On hearing such good news, everybody yelled *hooray* again.

"There's only one more thing to do," said Fairy Marina. She opened her fan, and the fishbone jumped out of Princess Alice's pocket. It flew through the air and landed in the mouth of the noisy dog that lived next door. From that day on, the dog was silent. It never barked at nor bit the children again.

QUIZ (4)

1. Describe King Rainbird.
2. How many children did the king and queen have?
3. How old was their eldest child?
4. What was Fairy Marina wearing when she first met the king?
5. Why did Fairy Marina get angry when the king asked *why*?
6. What did the king give Princess Alice to eat?
7. What did Princess Alice do with the fishbone after eating the salmon?
8. Why did the queen fall to the ground?
9. How did Princess Alice wake the queen?
10. Why were there no cooks or cleaners?
11. What was Princess Alice's close friend, Little Lady?

12. Why was the king always angry?
13. What did Princess Alice do whenever the king was angry?
14. What happened to the young prince who was chased by a dog?
15. What happened to the baby prince?
16. How did Alice stop the young princes and princesses from crying when she was taking care of the baby prince?
17. Why did the king sigh?
18. What did Princess Alice wish for with the fishbone?
19. Who was waiting in the church garden?
20. What happened to the fishbone when Fairy Marina opened her fan?

KEY VOCABULARY

NOUNS

1. ***Bow:*** a knot tied with two loops and two loose ends
2. ***Canoe:*** a small boat with pointed ends
3. ***Carriage:*** a vehicle for carrying people or goods
4. ***Cornet:*** a musical instrument made of brass that is similar to a trumpet
5. ***Court:*** a place where a judge decides if a person is innocent or guilty
6. ***Criminal:*** a person who has broken the law
7. ***Fairy:*** a creature with magical powers
8. ***Fist:*** a hand with fingers curled inward
9. ***Honour (UK) Honor (US):*** a person's reputation for being good and honest

KEY VOCABULARY

10. *Jewel:* a valuable stone
11. *Lavender:* a scent/smell made from the purple flowers of the lavender plant
12. *Mayor:* the head/leader of a town or city
13. *Miracle:* an amazing and positive event that is not natural
14. *Pearl:* a hard, white, smooth stone found in an oyster
15. *Penalty:* punishment for breaking the law or doing something bad
16. *Pirate:* a person who attacks other ships at sea
17. *Plan:* a description explaining how to do something
18. *Politician:* a person who is selected to make/change laws for a country
19. *Pond:* a body of water that is smaller than a lake
20. *Prisoner:* a person who is not free
21. *Property:* an item, such as a car or a house, which belongs to a person
22. *Respect:* a good opinion or attitude toward somebody
23. *Rug:* a covering for the floor

KEY VOCABULARY

24. ***Silk:*** material made from fibres produced by the silkworm
25. ***Slice:*** a cut of food
26. ***Spice:*** a plant used to add flavour to food
27. ***Telescope:*** an instrument for looking at distant objects
28. ***Tornado:*** a strong windstorm that twists around and around
29. ***Treasure:*** a collection of valuable things
30. ***Trial:*** a meeting held in a court with a judge
31. ***Uniform:*** clothes worn to show a person's job/position/status

VERBS

1. ***Bandage:*** to put a bandage on something
2. ***Bark:*** the make a short, loud sound (especially dogs)
3. ***Behave:*** to conduct oneself in a certain way
4. ***Bite:*** to attack something with the teeth
5. ***Bow:*** to lower one's head to show respect

KEY VOCABULARY

6. ***Bully:*** to act aggressively and intimidate others
7. ***Chew:*** to repeatedly crush something with the teeth
8. ***Embarrass:*** to humiliate somebody and make them feel uncomfortable
9. ***Encounter:*** to unexpectedly meet somebody or something
10. ***Impress:*** to do something to give others a positive/favourable impression of oneself
11. ***Gamble:*** to play risky games (horseracing, casino, pachinko…) to win/gain money
12. ***Land:*** to come down from the air/sky to the ground
13. ***March:*** to walk with long and strong steps like a soldier
14. ***Munch:*** to make a crunching sound while eating
15. ***Nod:*** to move one's head up and down
16. ***Order:*** to tell somebody to do something
17. ***Pack:*** to put clothes or personal items into a bag/suitcase
18. ***Polish:*** to rub a surface until it becomes shiny and/or smooth

KEY VOCABULARY

19. *Pretend:* to use the imagination to behave like somebody or something else
20. *Punish:* to make somebody suffer for doing something bad
21. *Recover:* to regain physical health
22. *Refuse:* to say no when asked to do something
23. *Rescue:* to save somebody from a dangerous situation
24. *Row:* to move a boat by pushing an oar through the water
25. *Rush:* to run/move fast/hastily
26. *Sail:* to use the wind to move a boat/ship through the water
27. *Sink:* to go down into the water/sea
28. *Scold:* to shout/yell at somebody for doing something bad
29. *Scream:* to shout/yell loudly
30. *Shave:* to remove hair with a razor
31. *Sigh:* to breathe out while making a sound (usually sad)
32. *Stare:* to look at something closely
33. *Sweep:* to use a broom/brush to make the floor clean

KEY VOCABULARY

34. *Throw:* to make an object/person move rapidly through the air
35. *Tie:* to wrap something/somebody with string/rope
36. *Whisper:* to speak softly/quietly
37. *Wrap:* to put material all around something or somebody
38. *Yell:* to speak loudly

ADJECTIVES

1. *Brave:* courageous / not afraid in a dangerous situation
2. *Coward:* not courageous / afraid in a dangerous situation
3. *Overweight:* unhealthily heavy
4. *Reasonable:* a good price / inexpensive
5. *Scared:* feeling fear
6. *Shocked:* surprised (usually by something negative)
7. *Stubborn:* refusing to do something in a different way
8. *Terrible:* unpleasant / very bad

9. *Trustworthy:* can be trusted / reliable
10. *Wise:* to have knowledge and/or experience

INTERJECTIONS

1. *Heave-ho:* something sailors say when they are pulling a rope
2. *Hooray:* something people say when they are happy, appreciate and/or like what somebody has said or done

ANSWERS

QUIZ (1)

1. William Tinkling meet his wife, Nettie Ashford, at dance school.
2. Robin Redforth got married to Alice Rainbird in the dance school closet.
3. Robin let off a firework to celebrate his marriage to Alice.
4. Nettie and Alice were staying with Ms. Grimmer and Ms. Drowvey.
5. Robin attacked Ms. Grimmer and Ms. Drowvey to free Nettie and Alice.
6. Robin was hiding a paper knife under his jacket during the attack.
7. Ms. Drowvey wrapped Robin's black flag around his head during the attack.

ANSWERS

8. William quietly waited behind the streetlight during the attack. He was following orders.
9. Robin's plan failed because Ms. Drowvey had refused to fall down.
10. "Is my husband a cow?" was written on the piece of paper that Nettie gave to William.
11. The Emperor of France had to escape over the back-wall of his garden to attend the trial.
12. The President of the United States of America was the judge during the trial.
13. The judge ordered the guards to put leaves into Richard's mouth.
14. The trial ended early because the Emperor of France's aunt marched into court, grabbed him by the hair, and took him home.
15. In the evening on the day after the trial, William, Robin, Nettie and Alice returned to the place where the trial had been held.
16. Nettie and Alice said that they needed to stop pretending because the adults would not do what they should do.

ANSWERS

17. Alice said that Robin would have his hair, ears, or nose pulled if he went to her house and claimed her.
18. Nettie said that William would have things dropped on his head from the window if he went to her house and claimed her.
19. They drank cherry-wine to celebrate their love.
20. William and Robin stayed under the willow tree after Nettie and Alice had gone home because their eyes were red from crying. They were embarrassed.

QUIZ (2)

1. Children ordered adult-children to make jam, jelly, cakes, pies, and desserts.
2. Adult-children were made to sit in a corner of the room if they didn't do as they were told.
3. Ms. Lemon was the principal of the school for adult-children.

ANSWERS

4. I think adult-babies have so few teeth because…(answers vary)
5. Ms. Orange and the school principal put their adult-babies on the rug while they were talking.
6. Ms. Orange took care of her parents, two of their close friends, one uncle, three aunts, and her adult-baby.
7. Mr. White was made to stand in the corner of the room because he had been gambling.
8. Mr. Brown's serious problem was greediness. He ate and drank too much.
9. The principal said that the worst thing adult-children did was bullying.
10. For lunch, Ms. Orange ate some sweet stuff, a dish of sweet bread, and sweet dessert.
11. Ms. Ali and Mr. Orange ate lunch with Ms. Orange.
12. Ms. Ali had decorated her living room with paper flowers.
13. Mr. Orange said that adult-girls think that they are more important than everybody else.

ANSWERS

14. Ms. Ali prepared salmon, salad, and roast beef for the adult-children to eat.
15. The first adult-child to arrive at the party wore glasses and was overweight.
16. The adult-boys who were standing in the doorway were talking about newspapers.
17. Ms. Ali sent the adult-boy with a beard home early because he was standing on the rug in front of the fire warming his back.
18. The band played the harp, the cornet, and the piano.
19. The adult children who were making speeches were pretending to be politicians.
20. The adult-children were sent to school during the holidays.

QUIZ (3)

1. Captain Braveheart become a pirate because his Latin teacher scolded him for no reason and then refused to fight him.
2. Captain Braveheart's ship was called *The Beauty*.

ANSWERS

3. Captain Braveheart caught a whale in the South China Sea.
4. During the two weeks when *nothing special happened*, the sailors captured four Spanish ships and one South American ship.
5. Bill Boozey was unhappy about the tea because the milk was the worst he had ever tasted.
6. When Bill Boozey was telling the captain about the tea, he stepped backward and fell into the sea.
7. The ship in the harbour was called *The Scorpion*.
8. The Latin teacher was the captain of the ship in the harbour.
9. The cook ran toward the Latin teacher with a cooking knife in his hand because he was angry that his brother had been killed in the battle.
10. Captain Braveheart killed the cook to stop him from attacking the Latin teacher.
11. After Captain Braveheart put the Latin teacher in a boat, he gave him a compass, a bottle of alcohol, a bottle of water, a piece

ANSWERS

of pork, a bag of biscuits, and his Latin grammar book.

12. Thunder, lightning, hurricanes and tornadoes continued for approximately three and half months.
13. The natives that approached *The Beauty* in canoes wanted to chew, munch and eat the sailors.
14. Captain Braveheart found the Latin teacher in the natives' village.
15. The sailors cheered when Captain Braveheart told them they were going to sail to England.
16. The captain's mother, father, aunts, uncles and cousins were on *The Family*.
17. The sailors threw the Latin teacher into the sea because he was behaving dishonestly.
18. The sailors locked the captain's cousin, Tom, in a room because he was behaving badly.
19. Captain Braveheart sailed to Margate to save his bride, Alice Rainbird.
20. The mayor rang the harbour bells to tell the

ANSWERS

captain that Alice's family had agreed to let her marry him.

QUIZ (4)

1. King Rainbird was strong, brave, and handsome.
2. The king and queen had nineteen children.
3. The king and queen's eldest child was seven years old.
4. Fairy Marina was wearing a silk dress when she first met the king.
5. Fairy Marina got angry when the king asked *why* because adults were always asking *why*.
6. The king gave Princess Alice salmon to eat.
7. After eating the salmon, Princess Alice dried, rubbed and polished the fishbone.
8. The queen fell to the ground because her head hurt.
9. Princess Alice woke the queen by holding a jar of strong smelling herbs under her nose.
10. There were no cooks or cleaners because the king was too poor to employ them.

ANSWERS

11. Princess Alice's close friend, Little Lady, was a doll.
12. The king was angry because Princess Alice didn't use her fishbone to make the queen better.
13. Whenever the king was angry, Princess Alice ran to her room to talk to Little Lady.
14. The young prince who was chased by a dog fell and cut his hand on some glass.
15. The baby prince fell down the stairs and injured his eye.
16. Alice stopped the young princes and princesses from crying when she was taking care of the baby prince by teaching them how to make soup.
17. The king sighed because he was very, very poor.
18. Princess Alice used the fishbone to wish for money for her father, the king.
19. Prince Robin was waiting in the church garden.
20. When Fairy Marina opened her fan, the fishbone jumped out of Princess Alice's pocket, flew through the air, and landed in

the mouth of the noisy dog that lived next door.

NOTE FROM THE PUBLISHER

At MATATABI PRESS, we're always looking for new talent. Contact us at the email, below, if:

1. You're a writer with a story to tell;
2. You're an EFL/ESL professional interested in working on an English graded reader;
3. You're a Japanese Language specialist interested in working on a Japanese graded reader; or
4. You're a Japanese-English translator interested in translating one of our publications.

Email: press@matatabi-japan.com
https://www.press.matatabi-japan.com/

NOTE FROM THE PUBLISHER

Matatabi Readers are graded by *sentence complexity* and *headword count*.

Sentence Complexity

Sentence Complexity Level	Flesch-Kincaid Grade Level
400	1 to 2
500	2 to 3
600	3 to 4
700	4 to 5
800	5 to 6
900	6 to 7
1000	7 to 8
1100	8 to 9
1200	9 to 10
1300+	10+

NOTE FROM THE PUBLISHER

Sentence complexity is calculated using the Flesch-Kincaid Grade Level Formula. Grade Level "3 to 4" (Level 600), for example, indicates that the sentence complexity is suitable for students in the third and/or fourth grade of school in the U.S.

Headword Count

Headword Level	Headword Count
D	301 to 400
E	401 to 500
F	501 to 600
G	601 to 700
H	701 to 800
I	801 to 900
J	901 to 1000
K	1001 to 1100
L+	1101+

NOTE FROM THE PUBLISHER

The headword count in a Matatabi Reader represents the number of words with separate definitions. That is to say, even if a word, such as *ship*, appears on every page in the book, it only represents one headword. Likewise, verbs and adjectives in all their forms are counted as single headwords. For example:

1. Eat, ate, eaten, and eating represent one headword; and
2. Tall, taller, and tallest represent one headword.

NOTE FROM THE PUBLISHER

MATATABI TRANSLATION SERVICES
https://www.translate.matatabi-japan.com/

English Editing
(<u>edit@matatabi-japan.com</u>)

Essays, Research Articles, MA Theses, Doctoral Theses, Conference Presentations, Business Emails, Sound Files, Websites, Materials for Publication...

Japanese-to-English Translation
(<u>translate@matatabi-japan.com</u>)

Film Subtitles / Audio Visual Translation (SRT, DFXP, SBV, SSA, TXT, VTT), Business Emails, Essays, Research Articles, Conference Presentations, Websites, Picture Books, Materials for Publication...

EDITORS

Josh MacKinnon (Adaptation)

Josh is an experienced Japanese-English translator, checker and proofreader. He is based in the UK and specializes in website and advertising material translation.

John McLean (Series Editor)

John is an associate professor at Yasuda Women's University in Hiroshima, Japan. He oversees the Department of English Interpreting Stream. He is known for his interpreting work with some of Japan's leading athletes and film directors. In 2020, he subtitled Toshihiro Goto's award winning film "Hiroshima Piano" [*Okasan no Hibaku Piano*].

www.ingramcontent.com/pod-product-compliance
Lightning Source LLC
Chambersburg PA
CBHW071530080526
44588CB00011B/1627